7000408492

KU-614-829

R-26 543
U.W.E
- 6 JUN 2007
Library Services

Whan that Aprille with his schowres swoote
The drought of Marche hath perced to the roote,
Thanne longen folk to gon on pilgrimages.
And specially, from every schires ende
Of Engelond, to Canturbury they wende.

The Franklin's Tale P32

The Clerk's Tale P30

The Summoner's Tale P28

The Wife of Bath's Tale P24

The Reeve's Tale P20

The Miller's Tale P16

Marcia Williams and Walker Books would like to thank
Dr Lesley A. Coote for the use of her edited
Wordsworth Canterbury Tales.

First published 2007 by Walker Books Ltd
87 Vauxhall Walk, London SE11 5HJ

10 9 8 7 6 5 4 3 2 1

© 2007 Marcia Williams

The right of Marcia Williams to be identified as author/illustrator of this work has
been asserted by her in accordance with the Copyright, Designs and Patents Act 1988

This book has been typeset in Stone Print Roman

Printed in China

All rights reserved. No part of this book may be reproduced, transmitted or stored in
an information retrieval system in any form or by any means, graphic, electronic or
mechanical, including photocopying, taping and recording, without prior written
permission from the publisher.

British Library Cataloguing in Publication Data:
a catalogue record for this book is available from the British Library

ISBN 978-0-7445-7007-6

www.walkerbooks.co.uk

The Pardoner's Tale
P36

The Nun's Priest's Tale
P40

FOR ABEL, GREET CHEERE!

Here bygynneth

Chaucer's Canterbury Tales

RETOLD AND ILLUSTRATED BY

MARCIA WILLIAMS

The Knight's Tale
P10

Chaucer's Greeting
P6

1½ MILES TO LONDON

WALKER BOOKS
AND SUBSIDIARIES

LONDON · BOSTON · SYDNEY · AUCKLAND

GEOFFREY CHAUCER
c.1340–1400

A KNIGHT
A WORTHY MAN

A MILLER
A STOUT CARL

A REEVE
A COLERIK MAN

A GOOD WIFE OF BATH
BOLD WAS HIR FACE

It was spring and I had met with a group of fellow pilgrims at Southwark, in the City of London. We planned to spend a night at the Tabard Inn before beginning a pilgrimage to Canterbury, several days' ride away.

Tabard Inn

A SUMMONER
OF HIS VISAGE CHILDREN
WEREN AFERD

A CLERK OF OXFORD
HE WAS NOT RIGHT FAT

A FRANKLIN
WHIT WAS HIS BERDE

A PARDONER
HEER AS YELWE AS WEX

A NUN'S PRIEST
I BE MERY!

We planned to visit the shrine of the martyr Saint Thomas Becket, a holy man, cruelly murdered by knights of Henry II in 1170. His body rests in the cathedral at Canterbury and his tomb is a most sacred place.

Ye ben to me right welcome hertily!

Oh, stories, goodie!

I hope they are crackers!

Bound to be, with this lot!

If they ever wake up!

Once our ponies were stabled we made merry with the help of our host, Harry Bailey. Harry was to accompany us on our pilgrimage and had thought of a plan to make the journey pass most pleasantly. He proposed that each pilgrim should tell a story on the journey; the best would be rewarded with a meal paid for by the rest.

Early the next morning, Harry gathered us together for the start of our journey. Some of us were still half-asleep, but eventually we were all awake and ready to start on our way!

Later that day we reached a watering place where we paused to draw lots to decide who should tell the first tale – the lot fell to the knight.

A tale with a tower, perfet!

All great tales have towers!

And dukes and birds!

And prisoners of fate!

No ranceoun!

The governor of Athens, in Ancient Greece, was a noble duke called Theseus. He lived in a palace with his wife, Hippolyta, and her pretty, freedom-loving sister, Emily, who never wished to marry.

Palamon and Arcite, two royal cousins from the kingdom of Thebes, were imprisoned near the palace in a tower. Theseus was determined never to free them, as Thebes and Athens were bitter enemies.

YEAR — BY — YEAR — AND — DAY — BY — DAY

Season followed season while Palamon and Arcite pined for their freedom. Their only comfort was their close companionship; they grew to be more like brothers than cousins. One May morning, however, something quite unexpected happened to change both their fate and their feelings for each other.

Palamon was woken by the sound of singing and on looking down into the garden below, he saw Emily. He let out a cry; in the morning light Emily resembled a goddess and he worshipped her instantly.

Arcite peered from the window to see what had caused his cousin's cry. He too saw Emily and gasped. First her beauty had captured Palamon's heart, now Arcite was also its prisoner.

Now certes, fals Arcite, thou schal not so!

Thou schalt be rather fals than I!

In an instant their kinship had turned to rivalry and jealousy. Where once they had passed their days in peace, they now argued over Emily, a lady whose love neither man had the freedom to win!

What about romance?

Thwarted romance is best.

Well, it's all here!

That'll mean trouble!

Eche man for himself!

11

The cousins continued to quarrel until Perotheus, Theseus' greatest friend, came to visit him. Perotheus had known Arcite as a child and begged his friend to let Arcite return home to Thebes. Eventually, Theseus agreed, but only on condition that if Arcite ever returned to Athens, he would forfeit his life.

Arcite was not at all happy to have gained his liberty. Imprisoned in Athens he could watch Emily from a window. In Thebes she was a painful memory.

Back in Athens, Palamon was consumed with envy. He was quite convinced that Arcite would raise an army and return to claim Emily as his bride.

For nearly two years both men lived alone and in torment, Palamon still confined to the tower and Arcite exiled in faraway Thebes.

Then one night Arcite woke up with the conviction that he must end his suffering by returning to Athens, even at the risk of being killed by Theseus.

Arcite went unrecognized in Athens and was able to work for Theseus. He saw Emily every day and he soon became a loved and trusted servant.

Palamon was now in his seventh year in the tower and at his wits' end. Then one night he managed to drug his gaoler and escape to the nearby wood.

Emelye!

Next morning, Palamon, who was hidden in the undergrowth, was woken by Arcite who was out riding and dreaming aloud of the beautiful Emily.

Fired by years of pent-up emotion, Palamon angrily leapt on Arcite and dragged him from his horse. The two cousins were soon fighting like wild boars.

By mighty Mars...!

Theseus, who was out hunting, heard the commotion. He recognized the culprits and condemned both men to death. Hippolyta and Emily were distraught.

The god of love – a, benedicite!

They persuaded Theseus to release Arcite and Palamon, so that each could raise a company of soldiers and return to fight for Emily's hand.

What took him so long?

Finding his courage.

His anger isn't lost.

He's playing it cool.

One year later Palamon and Arcite rode into Athens, each with a hundred brave and chivalrous knights.

Dooth nowe your devoir, yong knightes proude!

And nought to ben a wyf...

He wilneth no destruccioun of blood!

God save such a lord, that is so good!

Even Emily, who was still reluctant to be married, was impressed by the strength of their devotion. On the day of the tournament the stadium was packed, and when Theseus declared there was to be no killing, the cheers hit the sky. All day the two sides fought, none more bravely than Palamon and Arcite. Then, just as the two came face to face, Palamon was wounded by one of Arcite's knights.

What is my "devoir"?

It's your duty.

Is fighting a duty?

Only in storybooks.

A noble story.

Theseus declared Arcite the winner, and to a loud fanfare he rode towards Emily. But his horse took fright and threw him to the ground.

As Arcite lay dying he made peace with Palamon, whom he commended to Emily, in case she ever changed her mind and decided to marry.

Everyone was shocked by the death of the noble Arcite and a huge funeral was arranged in his honour. Afterwards, Palamon, who had recovered from his wound, returned to Thebes in mourning.

For several years the hostility between Thebes and Athens continued. Then, at last, Duke Theseus grew so weary of the conflict that he begged Palamon to return to Athens, marry Emily and unite the two states. Palamon was delighted when Emily made no objection, so they were married with much merriment. They, and the people of Thebes and Athens, then lived together very happily, without a single cross word – or so it is told!

UWE LIBRARY SERVICES

In Oxford there lived an elderly carpenter named John. He had recently married a young and beautiful girl called Alison, whom he adored. He guarded her with a jealous eye as she was only eighteen and very flirtatious!

Their lodger, Nicholas, a penniless student and astrologer, was smitten by Alison's youthful charms and longed to kiss her.

The parish clerk, Absolon, a rather prim but very stylish youth, who fancied himself as a musician, had also fallen for Alison's charms.

Absolon tried to win Alison's love by offering her valuable gifts, but she always met his adoration with mocking indifference.

Nicholas was too poor to offer gifts; he just offered his heart, over and over again, until Alison could resist him no longer.

Jealousy is a great sin.

So is coveting another's wife.

Sins must be paid for....

Medieval sinners, BEWARE!

John was very suspicious of the young pair and kept a close eye on them. So Nicholas was forced to devise a plan so that he could spend time alone with Alison.

He told John that the stars forecast a great flood. He said that they must hang barrels from the rafters, so they could all float on the floodwater like Noah.

John was blinded by his fear of losing Alison and believed the rogue! The following Monday he fixed three wooden barrels to the rafters and provided each with food, drink and an axe. That evening, when all was quiet, Alison, John and Nicholas climbed into their barrels and waited for the floodwaters to come!

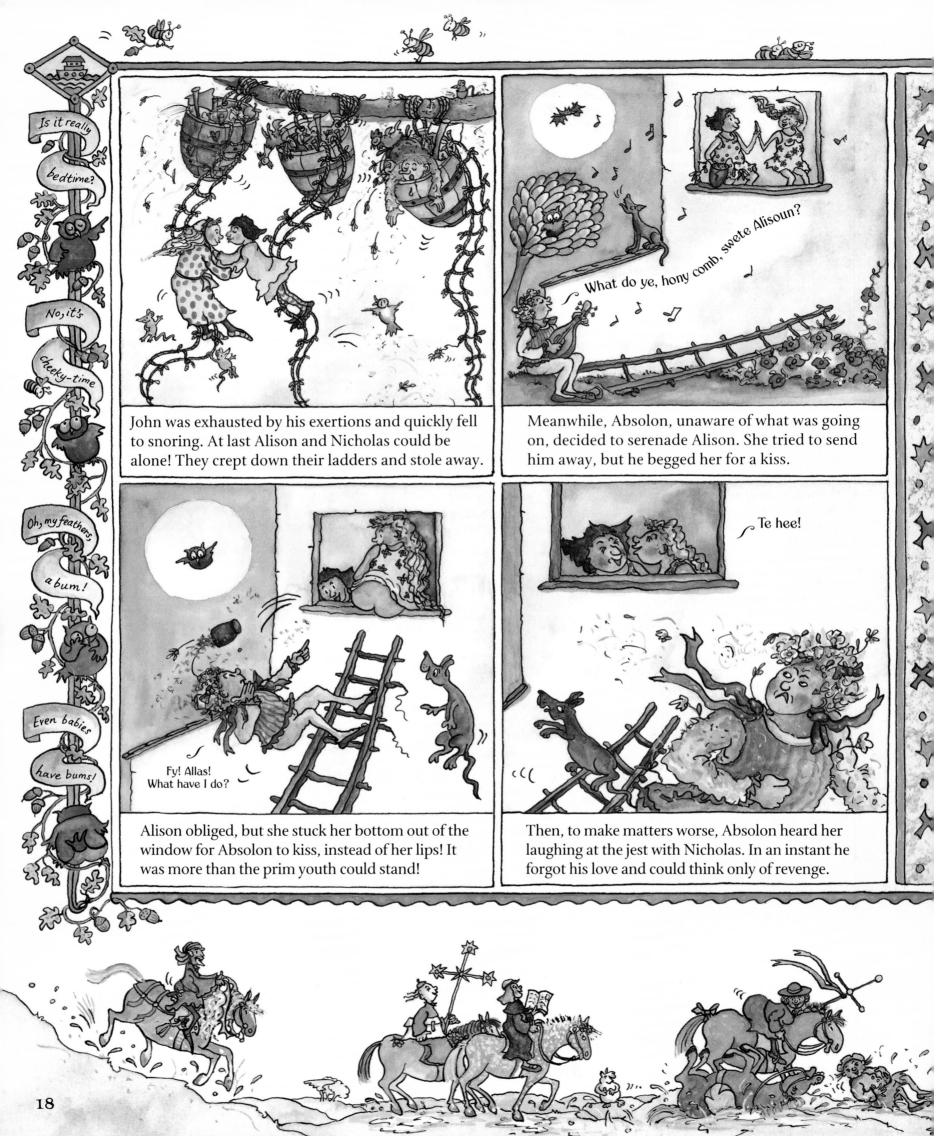

Is it really

bedtime?

No, it's

cheeky-time

Oh, my feathers,

a bum!

Even babies

have bums!

John was exhausted by his exertions and quickly fell to snoring. At last Alison and Nicholas could be alone! They crept down their ladders and stole away.

What do ye, hony comb, swete Alisoun?

Meanwhile, Absolon, unaware of what was going on, decided to serenade Alison. She tried to send him away, but he begged her for a kiss.

Fy! Allas! What have I do?

Alison obliged, but she stuck her bottom out of the window for Absolon to kiss, instead of her lips! It was more than the prim youth could stand!

Te hee!

Then, to make matters worse, Absolon heard her laughing at the jest with Nicholas. In an instant he forgot his love and could think only of revenge.

Help! Watir! Watir! Help, for God's herte!

This wol I give the, if thou me kisse.

Absolon dashed to the local forge and returned with a red-hot iron. He then begged Alison for one last kiss, in return for a precious ring.

This time, Nicholas stuck his bottom out of the window, while letting fly a fart! Absolon almost fainted, but still branded the proffered backside!

He was agast and feerd of Noe's flood!

Allas! For now cometh Noe's flood!

Nicholas howled for water so loudly that he woke John, who, thinking the flood had come, cut down his barrel. Instead of splashing into water, he crashed to the floor, breaking both the barrel and his arm. The neighbours rushed in to find John on the floor, muttering about Noah's flood. Alison and Nicholas persuaded them he had gone mad – how they all teased the poor carpenter! As for Nicholas, it was a long time before he could sit down and it was an even longer time before Absolon stopped scrubbing his lips after his attempt at kissing cheeky young Alison!

This tale is too rude!

Yes, but it's very funny.

And the sins are paid for!

It might be a winner!

This tale is doon, and God save al the route!

By God, right by the hoper wol I stande.

Than wol I be bynethe, by my croun.

A thieving miller...

two cocky students...

a cheeky daughter...

it's trouble!

Miller Symkyn lived near Cambridge with his wife, their tiny baby and a teenage daughter, Malyne. The Miller was a brutish, boastful man who was particularly proud of his ability to steal corn from the local college. At last, two students, John and Aleyn, decided to oversee the grinding of the corn and put a stop to his thieving.

The grettest clerks beth not wisest men.

Harrow, and weylaway! Oure hors is lost.

Allas, your hors goth to the fen!

Miller Symkyn was determined to outwit the students and left them guarding the college corn, while he crept outside to untie their horse.

When the students discovered they had been tricked they were furious. They would have to leave their corn alone with the miller and set off to catch their horse.

NO PEEKING

Get us som mete and drynk and mak us cheere, And we wol paye trewly at the fulle.

Quickly, the delighted miller stole some of their corn, which his wife kneaded into a corn cake. Then their daughter, Malyne, hid the cake.

It was evening before the students managed to catch their horse. The disgruntled pair had no choice but to pay Symkyn for food and lodging for the night.

Sey forth thi tale, and tarye nat the tyme! Lo, heer is Depford and it is passed prime.

That evening the miller's family stuffed themselves with the extra food and beer that the students had paid for. John and Aleyn grew angrier and angrier.

Then, when the family fell asleep, they emitted a storm of noises caused by their over-indulgence, making it impossible for Aleyn and John to rest.

Aleyn was beside himself with fury. He had been cheated, his food had been scoffed, and now he was being kept awake. He decided to get his revenge by snuggling up beside Malyne, the miller's precious daughter! John tried to warn Aleyn against such rashness, but he took no notice.

So John, not wanting to be outdone, waited until the miller's wife got up, then he moved the baby's cradle from the end of her bed to the end of his bed.

When the miller's wife felt her way back through the dark via the cradle, she unwittingly climbed into bed beside John, instead of her husband!

Farwel, Malyn, my sweete wight —
The day is come, I may no lenger byde.

At the first cock's crow, Aleyn felt it would be wise to return to his own bed before the miller woke and found him with his daughter.

John, thou swyneshed, awak!

Unaware that John had moved the cradle, Aleyn crawled into bed with Miller Symkyn and started to boast of his night spent with Malyne!

Symkyn rose up in a fury and punched Aleyn on the nose.

The pair fell upon each other like two grunting pigs in a sty.

Blow followed swiftly upon blow as both men vented their rage.

WHAM!

WHOP!

WALLOP!

Then, the miller fell backwards onto his sleeping wife.

She awoke in a daze and thought a thief was attacking her.

She grabbed a cudgel and whacked her husband over the head!

Cock-a-doodle-do!

They're fighting!

My beak, you're quick!

Allas and weylaway!

Aleyn and John took this opportunity to escape, but not before Malyne, who had fallen for Aleyn's charms, had given them back their corn cake. So the pair returned to college with the full quantity of corn, plus a merry tale to tell about how justice had been done and the cheating miller had been well thrashed!

Thus have I quyt the miller in his tale.

In the days of King Arthur, when all the land was filled with fairies and magic, a bold bachelor knight of Arthur's court went hawking.

As he returned to court, he came upon a fair maiden whom he treated with great cruelty. King Arthur would not tolerate such behaviour.

> What thing is it that wommen most desiren?

At court, the king sentenced the knight to death. The queen pitied the young knight, so she persuaded the king to allow her to choose his punishment.

The queen decided to send the knight on a quest. If he could discover what it is that women most desire, his life would be spared. How he sighed at this task.

> Yet wol I give the leve for to goon
> A twelf month and a day, it for to lere.

He had one year and one day to search for the answer; if he failed he would be beheaded. The young knight had no option but to take his leave of the queen and set off on his quest, however impossible it seemed.

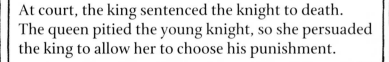

A handsome knight.

An impossible quest.

What will it mean?

A dead handsome knight!

The knight stopped at every place where he thought someone might know what it is that women most desire, but no two people ever agreed on the answer. As the months went by his heart grew heavier and heavier.

Finally, the day dawned when the knight had to return to the queen, even though he could not give her an answer. As he rode along the homeward track, he glimpsed a group of delightful damsels dancing in a glade. Eagerly he spurred his horse on, for surely one of them would know what women most desire.

As he drew close to the glade, the dancers vanished and an ugly hag was left sitting alone on the grass. In desperation the knight told her of his plight.

The hag smiled hideously, and told the knight that if he promised to do the first thing she asked of him, she would give him the answer.

The knight could not believe his luck, and although her ugliness repelled him, he lifted the old hag onto his horse and they set off for court. All the while she whispered her secret knowledge into his ear.

On the appointed day, the knight came before the queen and confidently told her that what women want most is to have command over their man.

In all the court there was not one lady who could contradict the knight. They were all delighted and declared that he deserved his life!

Bifore the court then, pray I the, Sir Knight, that thou me take unto thy wif.

Allas, and waylawey!

Yet the knight's relief was short-lived, for suddenly the old hag reminded him of his promise and demanded to be his wife!

For God's love, as chese a new request: Tak al my good, and let my body go!

The knight failed to persuade the hag to take his wealth instead, so the pair were married the next morning, without ceremony or celebration.

Thow art so lothly, and so old also.

The knight hated his wife. She was ugly, poor and of lowly birth. She told him that love was nothing without contentment and asked him to choose between having her young, beautiful and flirtatious, or old, ugly and for ever faithful.

For as yow likith, it suffisith me.

The knight, remembering the answer to the queen's riddle, told her to choose. At this the hag kissed her husband, and as she did so, she became both young and beautiful. His heart filled with love for her – and so it remained throughout their long and happy marriage!

She's cunning.

She's got him...

and his obedience.

She is a winner!

And thus thay lyve unto her lyves' ende In parfyt joye...

27

Friar John was a greedy and dishonest monk who travelled around Yorkshire, going from house to house, begging for food and money. In return he promised to pray for the sick, the dying and the needy. Many poor families gave him their last penny and crust of bread, but Friar John never said a prayer for one single soul.

One day, Friar John called on a family who had always been very generous to him, but Thomas, the father, was ill and refused to give him a penny. Thomas felt cheated. Over the years he had given all he could for the friar's prayers. Yet he had become sick, he was still poor, and worst of all, his baby had just died.

Thomas's wife still believed the friar's lies, even when he said he had seen their baby's death in a vision and that his prayers had carried the baby up to heaven.

Full of gratitude, she went to cook the friar a dinner that would leave her family hungry. Meanwhile the friar continued to try and wheedle money out of Thomas.

Beware of wheedlers.

Beware of liars.

Beware of greed.

Beware of Friar John!

28

Thomas, nought of your tresor I desire
For myself, but for oure covent.

The friar wept over his own poverty, the poverty of his fellow monks, and their crumbling monastery. Thomas shook with fury at the friar's pretend distress.

Now Thomas, help, for Seynte Charite!

Somwhat schal I give.

He longed to throw Friar John out, but instead promised him his last treasure, if it was shared equally amongst all the monks. The friar gave his most holy promise.

Thomas asked the friar to put his hand beneath his bum, where the treasure lay – then he let out a thunderous fart, one that any carthorse would be proud of. How Thomas laughed! The friar roared with anger, then ran to the local lord to seek retribution. Unfortunately for the friar, the lord ruled that Thomas must go to the monastery to provide another fart. Then all the monks could share it equally, just as Friar John had promised!

Something is brewing.

Maybe a winning line.

Or a winning treasure.

No, a winning fart!

We ben almost at toune.

29

Ah, wedded bliss... Will it last? She is too patient. Be Warned!

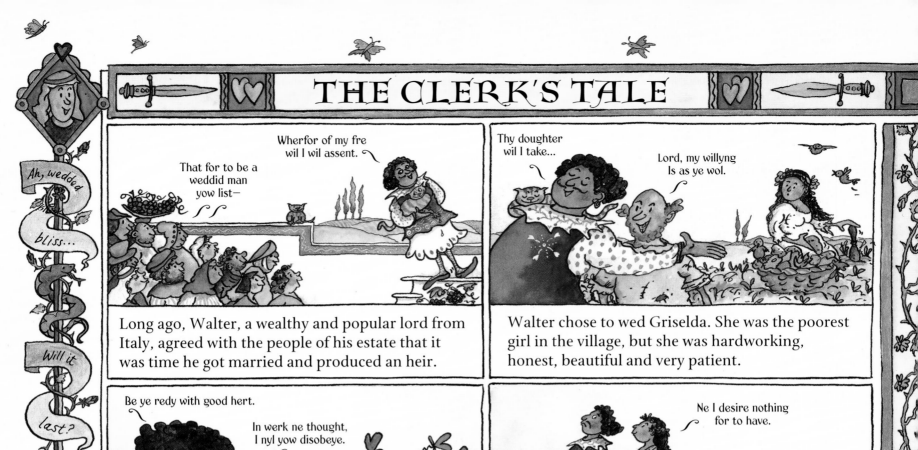

That for to be a weddid man yow list—

Wherfor of my fre wil I wil assent.

Long ago, Walter, a wealthy and popular lord from Italy, agreed with the people of his estate that it was time he got married and produced an heir.

Thy doughter wil I take...

Lord, my willyng Is as ye wol.

Walter chose to wed Griselda. She was the poorest girl in the village, but she was hardworking, honest, beautiful and very patient.

Be ye redy with good hert.

In werk ne thought, I nyl yow disobeye.

Griselda was delighted, and promised to be obedient to Walter in all things. She was a perfect wife and was loved by Walter and the local people.

Ne I desire nothing for to have.

After a few years the happy couple had a daughter. Walter began to be haunted by the idea that Griselda would love the baby more than him.

This child I am comaundid for to take.

Farwel, my child.

To test his wife, Walter sent a servant to take the baby. Although she feared her daughter would be killed, she obeyed Walter and gave up her beloved child.

Though that my doughter and my sone be slayn At your comaundement.

Some years later they had a son. Again, Walter tested Griselda by abducting the baby. Again, Griselda remained obedient to her husband.

I wil yow telle a tale which that I Lerned in Padowe of a worthy clerk.

I may not do as every ploughman may.

Walter was still not satisfied, so he told Griselda that he needed a new wife, one of noble birth. He sent Griselda home in nothing but her petticoat.

The chambres for t'array in ordinance.

A few days later, he asked Griselda to return and prepare the palace for his new bride and her brother. Griselda cheerfully set about the task.

How likith the my wif and hir beaute?

Right wel my lord.

She made Walter's future bride welcome and declared her to be the most beautiful girl she had ever seen.

This is ynough, Grisilde myn.

Finally, Walter realized that no wife could ever be more loving, patient or obedient to his wishes than Griselda.

He revealed that his new bride was really their daughter, and her brother, their son, both of whom had been living with his sister since their abduction. As she held her children in her arms, Griselda was overcome with relief. Walter declared his undying love and promised never to test her so cruelly again. He kept his word to her, just as she had always kept her word to him, and everyone rejoiced to see the family living in happiness and harmony once more.

He is a tyrant!

She is too patient.

This is not a winner!

Oooh... I don't know!

He's the fish's flippers! If he drowns he's mine. I'll have his toes! I'll save him!

Sire, I wol be youre humble, trewe, wyf.

Long ago, in Brittany, a young knight, Arveragus, courted the Lady Dorigen for so long and with such ardour that she finally agreed to marry him.

He was thrilled and on their wedding day vowed never to be jealous or insist on her obedience. In turn she promised to be a true and faithful wife.

SUMMER   AUTUMN
WINTER   SPRING

For nearly a year they lived together in perfect harmony.

Until Arveragus was called upon to go and fight overseas, in England.

Through lonely days and nights, Dorigen pined inconsolably.

Thise rokkes sleen myn herte for the feere!

She was afraid that her husband's ship would be smashed against the rocks that ringed the Brittany coast, and that he would drown and never return.

Her friends tried to distract her from this fear by arranging a picnic, but Dorigen would not be comforted, nor would she join their dancing.

At my bigynnyng first I yow biseche,
Have excused of my rude speche;
I lerned nevere rethorik, certeyn.

> Have mercy, swete, or ye wol do me deye!

Aurelius, a squire who had secretly loved Dorigen for years, observed her misery and was moved to declare his love, even though she was married.

> Ye remoeve alle the rokkes, stoon by stoon.

Dorigen was shocked! She told Aurelius she would be his love only if he removed every rock from the Brittany coast – confident it was impossible.

> Is ther noon oother grace in yow?

> No, by that lord that maked me.

Aurelius also realized the hopelessness of his task and all his dreams of being with Dorigen faded. He went home to nurse his broken heart.

Time passed and at last Arveragus returned home, without bumping into a single rock! He and Dorigen were happier than words could ever tell.

DORIGEN ♡ AURELIUS

Rokkes = impossible

Two years passed and all the while Aurelius, long forgotten by Dorigen, languished in bed, growing thinner and paler. Finally, he confided in his brother.

> My brother shal be warisshed hastily.

His brother was determined to help Aurelius and took him to Orleans, in France, to find a magician to assist Aurelius in winning Dorigen's love.

She may regret that.

Oh flip, he didn't drown.

We won't vote for this tale.

Not a scale's chance!

UWE LIBRARY SERVICES

What, no fish?

Poor, poor Dorigen!

It's just an illusion.

She doesn't know that.

There they found a magician who could fill a room with magical scenes. Aurelius was so impressed, he agreed to pay him one thousand pounds if he could conjure away the rocks from the coast of Brittany.

The following day they all left for Brittany, where the magician began to study the tides, the position of the moon and stars, and his books on magic.

After much study and thought he found a way to make it appear, for a while at least, that all the rocks had been washed away!

I have do so as ye comaunded me.

Allas! That ever this schulde happe!

Aurelius rushed to tell Dorigen and remind her of her oath. Her face turned pale; it was impossible for rocks to vanish from the sea, yet it had happened!

Ye schal your trouthe holden, by my fay.

Allas that ever was I born!

Dorigen wept as she told Arveragus the whole story. Though he pitied and loved her, he insisted that she keep her word to Aurelius and so retain her honour.

Dorigen went to Aurelius, but when he realized it was her husband who had sent her, he hesitated to embrace the wife of such a noble knight.

He decided that he must release Dorigen from her pledge, for to claim her love would only bring dishonour to him and unhappiness to all.

Dorigen fell to her knees and thanked him again and again.

Then she ran straight home and flew into the arms of her husband.

Never again were they divided, but lived in perfect happiness.

Poor Aurelius, both his purse and his arms were empty, so he asked the magician for more time to pay his debt. The magician was moved by the honourable behaviour of Aurelius, Arveragus, and his lady, Dorigen. So he released Aurelius from his debt, then mounted his horse and departed with his magical illusions.

35

One morning, in Flanders, three rowdy hooligans were sitting in a tavern, drinking and gambling, when they heard a funeral bell through the window. The publican's lad told them that a friend of theirs lay inside the coffin; a sneaky thief named Death had murdered him the night before.

The boy warned them to be on their guard, as Death hid around unexpected corners. Death had recently killed many villagers during a plague epidemic.

The ruffians were undeterred; they raised their beer mugs in brotherhood and swore to avenge their friend by finding Death and killing him by nightfall.

He schal be slayne, that so many sleeth!

They had no idea how they would recognize Death, but set off through the village full of drunken bravery.

Whi lyvest thou in so gret an age?

Lordynges, God yow se!

Before they had gone far they met a thin, bent old man. He greeted them most politely. However, the rude youths just asked him why he was still alive.

And deth, allas, ne wil not have my lif.

The old man told the hooligans that he felt tired and more than ready to die, but although he had pleaded, Death would not take him.

For in that grove I laft him, by my fay.

He scolded them for their rudeness and then said he had seen Death further along the path, by an oak tree.

Have you met Death? Not yet, but I will! Death has many guises. Too bloomin' many!

Now hold your pees — my tale I wol byginne.

37

Death is not there.

Don't be too sure.

Is Death a goodie?

Not as goodie as me!

This tresour hath Fortune to us given,
In mirth and jolyte our lif to lyven.

Today that we schuld have so fair a grace?

When the ruffians reached the tree they did not find Death, but several bushels of sparkling coins. All thoughts of avenging their friend vanished, as they persuaded themselves that the money was rightfully theirs!

This tresour moste caried be by night.

Rather than risk arrest, they decided to steal the coins under the cover of darkness, and drew lots to see who should go to the village for food and wine.

The lot fell to the youngest of the three and he set off in high spirits, imagining how he would spend his share of the money.

And I schal ryf him thurgh the sydes tweye
Whils thou strogelest with him, as in game!

Meanwhile, the other two thought how fine it would be to split the money between them. So they plotted to trick their friend into a fight and then kill him!

O Lord, if so were that I might
Have al this gold unto my self alloone.

The youngest also thought it was a shame to share the money, so he decided to kill his two friends by adding poison to their bottles of wine!

PARDONS FOR SALE

O cursed synne, ful of cursednesse!
O traytorous homicidy! O wikkednesse!

38

When he returned to the tree, one friend engaged him in playful wrestling, while the other stabbed him to death, just as they had planned.

Now let us drynk, and sitte an make us mery.

They celebrated their wicked deed before settling down to wait for nightfall. Unfortunately for them, they drank the poisoned wine and died instantly.

So it was that all three found Death under the oak tree – but not quite in the way they had expected!

This tale is scary!

Can we turn the page?

No, we need a winner.

Death is the winner!

In the left margin, on a scroll: *We still speak, tweetie!* *Fluff me, what a voice!* *And he knows it.* *He's a cocky cock!*

In days long past when animals could speak and sing, a poor widow lived in a tiny farm cottage near to a meadow and a wood. She shared the smallholding with her two daughters, three pigs, three cows, a sheep and a cock called Chanticleer, who had seven wives. Chanticleer was famous throughout the land for his fine voice.

My lief is faren on londe.

Chanticleer's favourite wife was a pretty hen called Pertelote. Every day they would greet the dawn together with a song in perfect harmony.

Herte deere, What eylith yow to grone in this manere?

Until one morning when, before dawn had risen, Chanticleer began to moan and groan so loudly and with such distress that he woke up Pertelote.

By God! Me mette I was in such meschief Right now, that yit myn hert is sore afright!

Away! Fy on yow, herteles!

He told her that he had dreamt that an orange beast had come into the yard to kill him, and now his heart was fluttering with fear!

For God's love, as tak som laxatyf!

Pertelote scoffed. She told Chanticleer that his nightmare was due to overeating! He assured her that it was not, and that every dream has a meaning.

Com ner, thou prest; com ner, thou Sir John
Tel us such thing as may our hertes glade;
Be blithe, although thou ryde upon a jade!

Then Chanticleer told Pertelote this sad tale of a man who foolishly ignored the warnings of his dreams:

Two friends were journeying together when they reached a busy, crowded town.

That night they had to take separate lodgings, one in an inn, the other in an ox's stall.

The man in the inn had a terrible dream, in which his friend was about to be murdered.

He woke in terror, but as it was only a dream he dismissed it and decided to go back to sleep.

Then he woke again, after dreaming that his friend was crying out for his help!

Again he slept, and this time he dreamt that his wretched friend had already been murdered.

His friend begged him to rescue his body, now hidden in a dung cart, and avenge his death.

The next morning the man found his friend's ox stall bed empty. He went to the town's western gate.

There, just as he had seen in the dream, he found a cart loaded with dung.

He called a guard and under the dung they discovered the body of his murdered friend.

The guard arrested the carter and the man rescued the body of his murdered friend.

If only he had taken proper notice of his **first** dream, his friend might **still** have been alive.

Yis, sire; yis, hoste, al so mot I go,
But I be mery, y-wis, I wol be blamed.

She's a
hard hen!

I'd give him
a cuddle.

Cocky by name
and nature

Not for much
longer!

...tak some laxatyf!

Now let us speke of mirthe.

Womman is man's joye and man's blis.

Pertelote remained unconvinced. She was sure that her husband just had indigestion and Chanticleer loved her too dearly to keep arguing.

He jumped down from the straw and calling all his wives to follow, strutted about the yard pecking at the corn and listening to their loving clucks.

Ful is myn hert of revel and solaas.

Cok, cok!

As the morning went on, Chanticleer forgot his dream and all its fears. Spring was in the air, his precious Pertelote was at his side and he was happy.

Then, suddenly, a beautiful butterfly in the cabbage patch caught his eye, and then, hidden among the rows of cabbages, he saw a bright orange fox!

Be ye affrayd of me, that am youre frend?

Chanticleer was about to run, but the fox insisted he was Chanticleer's friend and had come to hear his singing, which was the talk of every farmyard.

Chanticleer was proud of his voice and he was easily flattered, so he agreed to sing a verse. He shut his eyes, stretched out his neck and then ... the fox pounced!

Out, harrow, and wayleway!
Ha! Ha! The fox!

It grabbed Chanticleer by the neck and fled across the meadow towards the wood, with the whole farmyard in pursuit!

Thou schalt no more, thurgh thy flaterye,
Do me to synge and wynke with myn ye.

As they reached the wood, Chanticleer managed to control his fear and suggest to the fox that as he was now safe from capture, he should tell his pursuers that they might as well go home. The fox was tired of running and, without thinking, opened his mouth to reply – setting Chanticleer free! He flew quickly up into a tree. The fox tried to flatter him back to the ground, but this time Chanticleer was not going to let vanity get the better of him. He looked down and crowed triumphantly at the orange monster of his dream whom he had outwitted!

Even a fox must eat.

I recommend corn.

Look behind you, Mr Fox!

Ssh! This is life, not theatre!

But ye that holde this tale a foyle
As of a fox, or of a cok, or of a hen –
Takith the moralite, goode men.

43

It's a miracle... They've arrived! But who's the winner? Everyone's a winner!

The last tale has now been told and we are approaching Canterbury. Since leaving London, we've travelled nearly 120 miles across open country, so it is comforting to hear the noise and bustle of a city again. It hasn't always been an easy or comfortable journey and I think we're all quite weary, our ponies too!

CHAUCER'S FAREWELL

It'll be the Knight!

"No, it's the Miller."

Rubbish it's the Clerk.

Sssh! Let the reader choose.

We plan to have a hearty meal and a good night's rest before visiting the shrine of Saint Thomas Becket. So far we've been unable to decide who will *not* be paying for their supper. Every tale has helped our journey pass quicker and I hope they have entertained you as you've travelled with us. Farewell, and blessings on you all.

GLOSSARY

belamy – good friend
dagoun – snippet
leere – learn
lothly – ugly
mette – dreamed
parlous – dangerous
ranceoun – ransom
rede – advise
route – company
ryf – stab
wende – walk or
would think